New Age Follies

A Critique of Gail Riplinger's "New Age Bible Versions"

Albert M. McIlhenny

New Age Bible Follies: A Critique of Gail Riplinger's "New Age Bible Versions"

Copyright © 2011

ISBN 978-1-257-79424-9

Albert M. McIlhenny

All Rights Reserved

Table of Contents

Introduction   7

Chapter 1 – You Can Quote Me On That   11
    How Gail Riplinger distorts the words of New Testament scholars

Chapter 2 – Prophets of a New Age?   21
    How Gail Riplinger misrepresented Westcott and Hort

Chapter 3 – Errors of Biblical Proportions   43
    How Gail Riplinger mishandles the text of Holy Scripture

Chapter 4 – The Catholic Menace   49
    Gail Riplinger's double standards in accusing modern translations of being "papist"

Chapter 5 – Acrostic Algebra and Revelation 57
Gail Riplinger's claims to special revelation

Chapter 6 – Manuscripts 59
A short survey of common KJV Onlyist errors in dealing with the manuscript tradition

Chapter 7 – Conclusion 63
Some final words

Appendix – Review 65
A review of "New Age Bible Versions" written for the website Christian Book Reviews (Christianbookreviews.net)

Bibliography 69

Introduction

For the last few decades, controversy has occasionally arisen within the Church over the place of the King James Bible. There is a belief, commonly called "King James Onlyism" or "KJV Onlyism" which states the King James Version of the Bible (KJV), sometimes called the Authorized Version (AV), is the one perfect Word of God and modern translations are rooted in a Satanic plot to undermine the truth of God's Word. One will find all sorts of wild claims outlining conspiracies traced over centuries and involving such luminaries as B. F. Westcott, Edwin H. Palmer, and Philip Schaaf along with Christians from antiquity such as Origen and Jerome.

The whole thing could be written off as an example of pop culture paranoia were a number of Christians not taking this drivel seriously. Videos abound on Youtube and similar outlets detailing the centuries old plot to suppress the Bible. In its most fanatical versions, this phenomenon not only claims the KJV is perfect but constitutes an improvement that corrects any Greek or Hebrew manuscript. Never mind the KJV relied in places on much later readings and at least in one place renders a conjecture by a sixteenth century scholar that appears in a total of zero New Testament manuscripts.[1] It is in the "perfect" Bible and everything else is a perversion of the Word of God.

One of the most popular apologia for this view is Gail Riplinger's *New Age Bible Versions* (henceforth NABV). Since its first publication in 1993, this hefty volume has become a favorite of many KJV Onlyists. Riplinger not only believes the new versions to be inferior but tools in a

---

[1] The KJV reading of Revelation 16:5 is based upon a conjecture by Theodore Beza that appears in no Greek manuscripts.

8 Introduction

worldwide satanic conspiracy to deny believers the true Word of God. More than any other defender of this view, NABV has popularized this misguided belief and convinced many Christian believers their once cherished Bibles were actually tools of Satan. Through sensationalism, poor scholarship, and deceptive presentations of the writings of Christian scholars, Riplinger weaves what could only be considered a mythology of Bible transmission that has little in common with actual history.

This booklet will not attempt to critique every single point Riplinger makes. That would in itself be giving it far more attention than it deserves. Rather, it will focus on whether, from a sampling of her key claims, Riplinger can be considered a trustworthy source. In particular, close attention will be paid to her use of quotations from scholars involved with modern translations. As will be demonstrated, her renderings of their words are often taken completely taken out of context or are manufactured for the sole purpose of making them appear to back positions they did not actually support.

The most egregious abuses of these scholars appear in her use of what one might call the "Magic Ellipsis." The ellipsis (...) is a well established notation for omitting sections of a quoted passage that are irrelevant to the subject under discussion. However, Riplinger often uses it to connect completely unrelated phrases from different pages and even different books! They are then arranged as though they were part of a single passage and their meaning completely distorted in the process. Such misuses are not merely sloppy notation but complete distortions of their views. This is a dishonest and disreputable practice and Riplinger must be held accountable for such blatant lies.

Even worse is her handling of the Bible. She often completely distorts the nature of the differences between the KJV and modern versions and makes the newer translations appear to be denying essentials of the Christian Faith when this is clearly not the case. Furthermore, she clearly has no understanding of the New Testament manuscript tradition apart from what she may have read in KJV Onlyist propaganda.

Introduction 9

Despite such shortcomings, Riplinger is often praised by her fans for her "scholarship." Given the evidence presented in this short booklet, even the bare minimal standards of scholarly integrity render such an evaluation quite laughable. NABV is the wild ramblings of a conspiracy theorist as she plays connect-the-dots with historical events and uses the historical transmission of the Bible as her own personal Rorschach blot. There is little in the way of evidence behind NABV and nothing in the way of scholarly integrity.

There will be those who might state nothing in this book "proves" the KJV is not the perfect Bible. This I can concede but the question of proper readings of the Holy Scriptures are not to be handled in a little booklet such as this. Rather the point here is to make those supporting the arguments used in NABV that they are staking their position on the words of someone who is blatantly dishonest. If they wish to continue to defend the KJV as perfect, that is certainly their right, but to do so with arguments that are fabrications brings their own favored translation into disrepute.

This is perhaps the greatest tragedy of the sort of bluster promoted by Riplinger and others like her. The King James Version of the Bible was a marvelous translation by pious scholars who sought to further the knowledge of God's Word with all their abilities and the information they had available to them. Their work deserves a treasured place in the hearts of Christians and these men deserve out utmost praise. However, to claim for the fruits of their efforts properties the translators themselves would have found blasphemous and to ascribe to them views far from those of seventeenth century Anglicans .

It is hoped that after reading this book, supporters of Riplinger and NABV will reexamine their position and check the evidence provided. Let them see for themselves the dishonesty with which she handled the work of New Testament scholars. Let them see for themselves her distortions of history. They might continue to assert the KJV as the perfect Bible if they wish, but let them not do so on the basis of the lies of Gail Riplinger.

10 Introduction

Chapter 1 – You Can Quote Me on That

Politicians often have their words come back to haunt them. The elder President Bush saw his promise "Read my lips: No new taxes!" backfire when he did raise taxes. With Gail Riplinger around, the same can happen to New Testament scholars. The only difference is the scholars in question may not remember writing what Riplinger used as their words.

The reason is not because of faulty memory on their part but because Riplinger has no qualms about taking isolated phrases from different chapters or even different books and stringing them together as though they were part of a single passage. Such pseudoquotations usually connect phrases that are not in any way relevant to the subject Riplinger is addressing. She merely connects them by the ellipsis (...) and treats them as though they are on topic and in the same passage. In other cases, she isolates a phase, treats it as a complete sentence, and in the process alters the meaning. The blatant dishonesty of such practices seems not to deter Riplinger at all. With all of her claims of things being removed from the Bible, one might think the commandment against bearing false witness had been removed from hers.

One barely turns a page when, in the introduction to *NABV*, we are greeted by the following quote from NIV Chief Editor Edwin H. Palmer:

> [F]ew clear and decisive texts that declare Jesus is God.[1]

This is a rather strange quote. In fact, it is not even a grammatically correct sentence. It does, however, give the impression Palmer is skeptical

---
1 *NABV*, 2.

12 Chapter 1 – You Can Quote Me on That

about the divinity of Jesus. This is further emphasized by a claim of the "NIV heresy" and, presumably, Palmer's as well. But is Riplinger accurate in her portrayal of this quote?

In actuality, Palmer is pointing out the KJV rendering of John 1:18 relied upon inferior manuscripts that clouded a clear assertion of Jesus' divinity. He notes there are only a few verses that explicitly assert the divinity of Jesus and this is one of those cases. However, the KJV rendering based upon later inferior manuscripts weakened this assertion in comparison to the clarity present in modern translations such as the NIV. Thus rather than denying the divinity of Jesus, as one might infer from Riplinger's misleading quote, Palmer was defending it.

The degree of manipulation present is made clear by comparing Riplinger's cited "quote" with the full sentence:

> John 1:18, as inspired by the Holy Spirit, is one of those **few clear and decisive texts that declare Jesus is God**. But, without fault of its own, the KJV, following inferior manuscripts, altered what the Holy Spirit said through John, calling Jesus "Son."[2]

Please note Riplinger isolated the phrase in bold and treated it as a sentence to make her point. In context, the meaning is completely different. Such blatant manipulation of the evidence could not be accidental.

Nor is this the only distortion of Palmer's article. In seeking to paint Palmer as an enemy of the KJV (and hence the Word of God itself), she quotes Palmer as follows:

> The KJV is misleading ... erroneous ... corrupted by errors.[3]

Reading the above citation, one would certainly believe Palmer had a

---

2 Edwin H. Palmer, "Isn't the King James Version Good Enough? (The NIV and the KJV Compared)" in ed. Barker (1986), 143.
3 *NABV*, 29.

Chapter 1 – You Can Quote Me on That

rather low opinion of the KJV. However, the first two sections of this supposed "quote" concerns how some words in the KJV whose meaning has changed since the seventeenth century can be misleading. The sheer dishonesty in Riplinger's mangling of the source is made clear by reading the original passage:

> **The KJV *has now obscure and* misleading *renderings* of** God's Word. This is so in part because some English words have changed their meanings since 1611. It is bad enough when translators have available only inferior copies of the original text of God's word but when, in addition to that, their translation of the Hebrew and Greek conveys **erroneous** ideas, the problem is compounded.[4]

Riplinger has changed the phrase "The KJV has now obscure and misleading renderings" to "The KJV is misleading." The actual phrase only speaks to how changes in the English language could lead to a misunderstanding of the translators' work. The word "erroneous" was not referring to the KJV but to possible misinterpretations due to such changes. Later, referring to manuscripts used by current versions, Palmer wrote:

> These ancient manuscripts were more reliable and accurate, not being **corrupted by errors** made during countless times of copying, such as occurred with the late manuscripts used by the KJV.[5]

Thus it is not the work of the KJV translators being called into question. Palmer is merely pointing out the limited range of manuscripts available to the KJV translators were generally late in the transmission process and had accumulated corruptions in the text over the centuries.

Riplinger then follows this up by quoting Palmer as accusing the KJV

---

4 Edwin H. Palmer, "Isn't the King James Version Good Enough? (The NIV and the KJV Compared)" in ed. Barker (1986), 143.
5 Edwin H. Palmer, "Isn't the King James Version Good Enough? (The NIV and the KJV Compared)" in ed. Barker (1986), 143.

Chapter 1 – You Can Quote Me on That

translators of misconduct:

> The King James Version ... changed the originals...[6]

In reality, this was taken from the discussion mentioned earlier concerning John 1:18 and referred only to that verse:

> A striking case of where the **KJV**, following bad Greek copies of the original text, **changed the** *original* in John 1:18.[7]

By removing the mention of the verse and Greek manuscripts used and then altering the word "original" to its plural form, Riplinger has presented a misleading inference concerning Palmer's opinion of the KJV.

If Riplinger wished to convey Palmer's true opinion of the KJV, she could easily have included his remarks that opened the article:

> I love the King James Version. I was converted under it, my first memory verses were taken from it, and I have been blessed by it. And God still uses the KJV to bring many people to salvation in Christ. This version was translated by godly men who did an excellent job with the tools they had in the language of four centuries ago. Countless millions have been converted, sanctified, and nurtured through it. Thank God for that marvelously used translation.[8]

Of course, when your intent is to accuse everyone attached to any modern version of being part of a New Age conspiracy, such "oversights" are to be expected.

Clouding Riplinger's treatment of Palmer is his standing as a theologian far better versed in the historical development of Christian doctrine.

---

6 *NABV*, 29.
7 Edwin H. Palmer, "Isn't the King James Version Good Enough? (The NIV and the KJV Compared)" in ed. Barker (1986), 143.
8 Edwin H. Palmer, "Isn't the King James Version Good Enough? (The NIV and the KJV Compared)" in ed. Barker (1986), 142.

Chapter 1 – You Can Quote Me on That   15

Riplinger often has no idea what point Palmer is actually making. So rather than doing the necessary research to comprehend his true intent, she chose to assume it was related to the occult. In the process, she only succeeds in making a fool of herself to anyone familiar with Palmer's work.

An example of this occurs when she quotes Palmer from his book on the Holy Spirit and infers he is denying the Protestant doctrine of *sola fide*:

> This [his own translation] shows the great error that is so prevalent today in some orthodox Protestant circles, namely the error that regeneration depends upon faith ... and that in order to be born again man must first accept Jesus as savior.[9]

Anyone familiar with Palmer know he did not deny sola fide. However, Palmer was a Calvinist and believed regeneration was an act of God's will producing faith in the elect rather than a free will choice of the redeemed. I will not here enter into a discussion of the merits of the Calvinist position but merely point out sola fide was not denied and Palmer's view was common among the Reformers. It is only Riplinger's historical ignorance that called his allegiance to the doctrine into question.

Lest we think Palmer was singled out, Riplinger quickly followed up this distortion with a misrepresentation of nineteenth century church historian, Presbyterian theologian, and ASV committee member Philip Schaff. She wastes no time connecting Schaff to the development of New Age theology by noting he encouraged altering the articles of faith:

> The changes thus far ... are in the right direction ... and should contain the germs of a new theology.[10]

So was Schaff advocating a denial of Christ's divinity? Or perhaps some sort of New Age pantheism? The "changes" occurring in the quote are not

---

9   *NABV*, 2.
10 *NABV*, 2.

16 Chapter 1 – You Can Quote Me on That

listed, the "right direction" not specified, and the "new theology" not outlined in Riplinger's excerpt. All we have are Riplinger's allusions to some New Age connections but, given her track record thus far, a closer examination is needed.

Not surprisingly, the quote in context has nothing to do with New Age influences. Presbyterianism is traditionally Calvinist but, under the influence of the "Great Awakenings," Presbyterians in America were replacing the Calvinist emphasis on predestination with the Evangelical emphasis on individual decisions for Christ. Schaff advocated adjusting official Presbyterian doctrinal statements to reflect this change and supported recent developments in that direction. Hence, when Schaaf is read in this context, the meaning is quite different from Riplinger's supposed discovery of occultic sympathies:

> **The changes** made **thus far** and communicated by you in confidence **are** judicious and **in the right direction**. The new sections on the Gospel and the Holy Spirit will be most important additions **and should contain the germs of *the* new theology** which has taken strong hold of the Presbyterian Church. The chapter on the Gospel will no doubt express its universal intent and the consequent duty of the church to offer it sincerely in God's name and to every human being made in His image. But this is inconsistent with the old historic Calvinism, which confines God's love and redeeming mercy to the circle of the elect, and leaves a great mass of men in the state of condemnation in consequence of Adam's fall. To make the revised confession consistent with itself, a number of passages, teaching expressly or impliedly the limitation of God's love and redemption, should be eliminated. We need a creed broad enough to embrace Toplady and Wesley and which clearly teaches both divine sovereignty and human responsibility.[11]

---

11 Schaff (1897), 427-428.

Chapter 1 – You Can Quote Me on That

Thus Riplinger performed a "cut and paste" that removed all content of the changes discussed and poured into these words the meanings created by her fertile imagination. She even replaced the definite article "the" in the phrase "germs of the new theology" with the indefinite article "a" to cloud the fact there is something missing afterward.

The net effect hides the real intent of endorsing a move away from a heavily Calvinist soteriology and replacing it with her own crackpot conspiracy theory. The great irony is King James Onlyists are generally anti-Calvinist and so Schaff is advocating something they support. But however one views the debate over Calvinism, the context clearly has nothing to do with "New Age" ideas.

Riplinger's assertions of a vast conspiracy seem to know no bounds. She assumes anyone associated with any modern translation is part of a vast New Age conspiracy and anything they have ever written is framed in that context. Early in the book, she claims the pressure to conform the Bible to the "One Word Religion" is conceded by insiders and supplies quotes to support her assertions.

One of those cited is Lewis Foster whose involvement with both the NIV and the NKJV made him a favorite target of Riplinger's brand of shoddy scholarship. For example, she unveils her "magic ellipsis" to form the following passage from his writings:

> Certain words have gathered theological significance through the years and to change them might be to change doctrine ... Do the changes in meaning come from new evidence or simply new theology.[12]

So does this passage reveal some secret plan by the Bible translating elite to subvert God's Word? In reality, it is not even a recognizable passage as the two sections are from completely different discussions and occur 55 pages apart! And the section she has as the conclusion is the one that appears 55 pages earlier! How can one claim to fairly represent someone's

---

12 *NABV*, 16.

18   Chapter 1 – You Can Quote Me on That

views without even maintaining any contextual integrity?

In fact, when one places the sections of this "passage" in context, Riplinger's quackery becomes self-evident. The opening portion of this "quote" deals with whether a Bible translation should use a special theological vocabulary or be in the common language of the day. Foster backed the latter idea and pointed out that a special vocabulary might cause one to read ideas into the text that are not the original intent. He summarizes his thoughts in this passage whose context has been completely distorted by Riplinger:

> Some would prefer that the Bible be kept different from other books in its form of expression. They prefer the classical Biblical way of putting things – identified with the King James Version. Still others are not as interested in the literary aspect as the theological. **Certain words have gathered theological significance through the years and to change them might be to change** the **doctrine**. Since, however, the New Testament was written in a contemporary Greek and not in a classical or special Biblical Greek, it should be translated into a contemporary English.[13]

Thus Foster merely advocated translating the Bible into the common language of the day and anticipated some possible objections. The passage had nothing to do with some imagined "One World Religion" and to claim such is dishonest and irresponsible. The latter half of this "quote" is equally misleading. Here the excerpt gives guidelines on judging translations. Foster stated those using less literal translations should check them against more literal ones, compare the differences, and note any doctrinal implications. Thus, in context, the second portion of the "quote" has nothing to do with any supposed One World Religion and is not even related to the first portion:

> Check a free translation against a literal translation, a new

---

13 Foster (1983), 76.

Chapter 1 – You Can Quote Me on That

translation against an old one. Are the differences changes in meaning or only changes in form? **Do the changes in meaning come from new evidence or simply new theology?**[14]

Riplinger's inference in this quote clearly has no connection with Foster's words in their original context. She has torn two sentences many pages apart from their original context, connected them with the ellipsis as thought they were in the same passage, and then supplied a new context for this nonexistent passage.

Riplinger further distorts Foster when she alleges he demanded readers use commentaries. She infers he is putting barriers between the Christian and the Word of God when she quotes him as follows:

> [I]t demands a good commentary to study the meaning of the passage.[15]

Here she has altered both Foster's words and the context of his suggestion. He was not addressing the average Christian reading the Bible but the methodology of Bible translators. He stated lexicons were not sufficient for a good translation since different contexts could support variant meanings and required translators familiarize themselves with different commentaries on the verses in question. Thus, in context, his stated:

> In actuality, the proper translation procedure requires several steps. The first is a rough translation recognizing the possibilities of the passages. Then when the exact meaning of the section is determined, the final translation will put the proper meaning in the best language to convey that meaning to the reader. ***This procedure*** demands ***the aid of*** good ***commentaries*** **to study the meaning of the passage.**[16]

---

14 Foster (1983), 21.
15 *NABV,* 50.
16 Foster (1983), 18.

20   Chapter 1 – *You Can Quote Me on That*

Riplinger replaced "this procedure" with "It" to hide the fact Foster was not addressing normal Bible reading. Once more we find Gail Riplinger has misrepresented the writings of others.

Another accused of buckling down to some supposed One Word Religion pressure is John Kohlenberger who Riplinger cites as asserting:

> [T]he question of a good or bad translation is no longer a linguistic one but a doctrinal one.[17]

So does this passage refer to some looming "One World Religion"? As might be expected, Riplinger has once more distorted the facts. In context, Kohlenberger was addressing the Living Bible paraphrase and noted such non-literal efforts were bound to include some of the doctrinal presuppositions of the translator.[18] But even worse, the quote she used is not Kohlenberger at all! The statement was quite clearly placed in quotation marks and cited from the Introduction to the Catholic edition of the *Living Bible*.[19] So not only does Riplinger twist her opponents' words to conform to her bizarre conspiracy theories, but she places in their mouths the words of others similarly twisted beyond all recognition.

The above passages are a small sample of the many distorted quotes supplied in NABV. Gail Riplinger is little more than an incompetent hack obsessed with conspiracy theories and lacking any real understanding of the writings of those she criticizes. As ridiculous as what has been presented thus far may be, it pales by comparison to the distorted quotes and meanings she uses to attack a pair of nineteenth century Anglican scholars: Brooke Foss Westcott and Fenton John Anthony Hort.

---

17 *NABV*, 16.
18 Kohlenberger (1987), 88-89.
19 Kohlenberger (1987), 89.

Chapter 2 – Prophets of a New Age?

As much as Gail Riplinger misrepresented Edwin H. Palmer and Lewis Foster, it pales in comparison to the histrionics she concocts against the nineteenth century Anglican scholars Brooke Foss Westcott and Fenton John Anthony Hort. As creators of the Westcott and Hort Greek New Testament that replaced the Textus Receptus, they were bound to attract Riplinger's attention. However, the degree of distortions and outright lies she aims at this pair of New Testament scholars from a century ago is breathtaking in its dishonesty. Since the publication of NABV, websites and other authors promoting KJV Onlyism have repeated Riplinger's claims without ever checking the original sources. Anyone is within their rights to criticize Westcott and Hort but to base this criticism on material that so completely fails to meet even minimal standards of fairness or accuracy is scandalous and undermines any claim to defend God's truth.

It does not take long in NABV for Riplinger to aim at Westcott, the better known of the pair, as she identifies him as a "spiritualist (one who seeks contact with the dead through seances), who believed he was in the 'new age.'"[1] Although she does not at this point supply evidence for his alleged spiritualism, she does give a reference for the "New Age" claim. However, when the source is checked, it merely is the use of the words "new age" in a speech he gave that had absolutely nothing to do with the current idea of "New Age" beliefs and Westcott was merely emphasizing the importance of Christians expressing the love of Christ to the less fortunate.

---

1 *NABV*, 2.

22 Chapter 2 – Prophets of a New Age?

In Westcott's day, many of the labor laws we now take for granted in the West were not yet enacted and the poor often lived in squalor. It was the consequences of the change in society through industrialization and the horrid living conditions of the working poor (immortalized in the novels of Charles Dickens) that Westcott referred to as a "new age" and not anything to do with occult practices.

Thus, reading Westcott in context, he points to signs Christians were beginning to understand the necessity of ministering to the less fortunate:

> ... signs that they are learning that the master-truth which is now brought home to us, that our possessions, our efficiency, our life itself, depend on others, must find active expression through the faith of Christ; signs that the co-operation of men widely different in character and place will manifest to the world the social power of the Gospel ; signs that once more in the face of unbelief and non-belief the Son of Man will vindicate His sovereignty by showing that He satisfies every need and every capacity which the struggles of a **new age** have disclosed.[2]

Does Riplinger seriously believe her distorted picture of his statement fairly represents his intent?

As distorted as her accusation here might be, her assaults on Westcott become progressively more hysterical. Using her "magic ellipsis," she mangles two quotes from completely separate contexts and presents them as one unified discourse on the alleged "New Age" deity she calls "the One":

> All ... is gathered up without loss in personality in One ...
> God in all things and all things in God.[3]

The first two parts of this "quote" come from Westcott's exegesis of the Apostles' Creed titled *The Historic Faith*. He was discussing the

---
2   Westcott, A. (1903b), 252.
3   *NABV*, 89.

Chapter 2 – Prophets of a New Age?

Communion of Saints and explained how the we as Christians are one body in Christ and yet this unity does not destroy our independent existence as persons. Thus, in context, the actual content of the passage is the exact opposite of New Age monism:

> It is, however, through such aspiration alone, quickened by the thoughtful study of that which the Spirit wrought in them, that we can enter into fellowship with their true life. Weaknesses, faults, errors, accidents of time and place, fall away. We learn to look upon the love, the courage, the faith, the self-sacrifice, the simplicity of truth which they embodied, and so become invigorated by vital contact with the eternal manifested through men. We rise, so far as we can rise under the pressure of earthly limitations, to some perception of the heavenly life, in which **all** that is personal **is gathered up without** the **loss of personality in One**, even ' in Christ.'[4]

The final part of the quote does occur in the pages of Westcott's writings twice but not in any of the pages referenced in the footnotes. It is odd, to say the least, that she cited no less than twelve pages[5] for a quote that only consists of three parts, with one of the three being a single word, and still managed to not cover the entire passage. Unless, she is pulling snippets of the last section from different pages, something that would make her crime against proper scholarship even greater, it occurs in either *The Historic Faith* or *Thoughts on Revelation and Life*. In the first case, Westcott described a reverence for God from seeing Him working through His creation[6] and in the latter he was emphasizing the importance of evangelizing India, then a British colony, and the words were clearly identified in connection with a *Hindu* prayer.[7] Neither had anything to do

---
4 Westcott, B. F. (1885), 256.
5 *NABV*, 656.
6 Westcott, B. F. (1885), 164.
7 Westcott, B. F. (1891b), 133.

24   Chapter 2 – Prophets of a New Age?

with the occultic intent Riplinger infers.

One must seriously wonder at this point if Riplinger has actually read any of this material or is merely culling sources from existing King James Only sources of questionable veracity. There is neither rhyme nor reason to her citations. Isolated phrases and even single words are ripped from paragraphs many pages apart and even from *different books* and presented as though they were part of the same discussion. Any author Riplinger opposes will likely have his original intent ignored as she manufactures "quotes" mimicking the words of known occultists. It doesn't matter if the phrases she assembles are from completely different contexts from both the occultist in question and each other. Faced with such complete deception on her part, no one can fairly look at her "scholarship" and do anything but shake their heads in disbelief.

Westcott and Hort are among those Riplinger portrayed as hardcore occultists. Her obvious motive is to undermine the credibility of modern translations by picturing them as satanic minions. This despite the fact no contemporary translation is based upon their text. As misleading as her cut and paste methodology might be, the truly disconcerting fact is many Christians (including some Christian leaders) have been so easily bamboozled by her brand of snake oil without ever seeing a need to substantiate her claims.

Perhaps the most memorable "quote" of Westcott conjured up by Riplinger's idiosyncratic brand of quotemining is this gem:

> [T]he revelation of the Divine in man realized in and through Christ ... Man is divine ... Every type of essential human excellence coexists in Christ ... humanity has been raised in the Son of Man to the right hand of God.[8]

Reading this "passage," you might think Westcott were making some sort of claim for human divinity. Riplinger would certainly love you to believe just that as she places it among quotes by New Agers, eastern mystics, and

---

8   *NABV*, 185.

Chapter 2 – Prophets of a New Age? 25

Word/Faith heretics. However, the sections of this "citation" do not occur in a single passage but are isolated phrases spread over *three separate books* strung together to appear they support something not part of their original contexts.

The first section is within Westcott's exegesis of John 17:22 where Jesus speaks of the glory the Father has given to the Son and this glory is given to those who follow Jesus. The opening of this so-called passage is actually the closing of a sentence where the revelation spoken of is clearly the Incarnation of God in the person of Jesus Christ and not anything pertaining to a general human divinity. This becomes abundantly clear when one reads the passage in context:

> This glory comes from the perfect apprehension of the Father as fulfilling His work of love (comp. *v.* 3). Viewed from another point of sight it is **the revelation of the divine in man realised in and through Christ**. So to know God as He accomplishes His will is to find all things transfigured; and as the Son of Man in His own Person experienced and showed the Father's purpose, so He enabled His disciples to appropriate the truth which He made clear.[9]

It is quite clear Riplinger cut off the beginning of the sentence to hide the fact the "revelation of the divine in man" was describing the Incarnation of Jesus Christ and had nothing to do with humanity in general.

The second section is from an exegesis of 1 John 2:18 speaking of the antichrist. The words "man is divine" does not represent the belief of Westcott but is presented as the "lie of antichrist." Westcott mentions the "divine destiny of man" as union with God through Christ. Such union is mentioned in Holy Scripture where, for example, Peter speaks of the promise of Christ as becoming "partakers of the divine nature" but such union does not entail ontological equivalence. The lie of antichrist is,

---

9   Westcott, B. F. (1882), 246.

26   Chapter 2 – Prophets of a New Age?

according to Westcott, that "man is divine." This is false, as Westcott points out, as man's only connection to the divine is in union with God through Jesus Christ. Any claim to an ontological divinity is the lie of antichrist. Thus, Westcott's true intent is made clear when seen in the original context and not through Riplinger's distortion:

> Under one aspect it may be said that the work of the Incarnation was to reveal the true divine destiny of man in his union with God through Christ; while the lie of Antichrist was to teach that **man is divine** apart from God in Christ.[10]

Note the complete distortion present from changing "the lie of Antichrist was to teach man is divine" to simply "man is divine." Such a blatant misrepresentation only further underscores the blatant dishonesty of her work.

When we get to the third portion of this quote, we are actually dealing with an exegesis of the Apostles' Creed that describes how Jesus Christ embodied all perfection in his union of divinity and humanity. Again the passage speaks only of Jesus in particular and not mankind in general:

> It is true, indeed, that **every type of essential human excellence coexists in Christ**, the Son of Man;[11]

The "convenient" omission of the phrase "the Son of Man" thus clouds the fact that this is a particular and not a general statement.

The final portion is again in the exegesis of the Apostles' creed and here is describing the work of the Holy Spirit. The quoted portion notes the Holy Spirit did not come in fullness to mankind until after the finished work of Jesus Christ in his passion, death, resurrection, and ascension to the Father. Thus the humanity taking a seat at the right hand of the Father is the humanity of Jesus and not mankind in general:

> But it was not till the full consequences of sin had been

---
10 Westcott, B. F. (1892), 70.
11 Westcott, B. F. (1885), 251.

borne and death had been conquered, and **humanity had been raised in the Son of man to the right hand of God**, that the rushing wind and fiery tongues told outwardly, at the festival of the gathered harvest, of the fulfillment of the promise of the Father.[12]

The examination of this supposed "passage", a Frankenstein monster of a quote assembled from four places in three books, makes quite clear Gail Riplinger is engaging in the most despicable form of quotemining imaginable and has absolutely no scholarly integrity. Even if one believed Westcott wrong or even heretical on issues, it does excuse such outright deception and reflects on her overall lack of concern for the truth.

When Riplinger turns to Westcott's supposed role as an occultist, her evidence is his membership in two clubs as a university student and one alleged but clearly erroneous connection to the Theosophical Society of the occultist Madame Blavatsky. Each of these items are played for far more than the evidence allows and her haranguing on these topics falls far short of rational. Any possible connection she can assert, no matter how trivial, counts as ironclad proof of Westcott's nefarious intentions.

The first, and perhaps the most serious evidence presented, was Westcott's involvement with something called the "Ghostly Guild" for investigating signs of the supernatural. It all seems very peculiar now but the idea of ghosts and spirits were all the rage in nineteenth century Britain and America. There were numerous claims of otherworldly phenomena being taken seriously by the intelligentsia of the time and a group of college students decided to investigate these claims. This could be written off as the sort of faddish lark that college students engage in but Riplinger sees the workings of a worldwide satanic conspiracy. The fact he has no evidence of this is no problem since she is obviously willing to manufacture quotes to fit her preconceived conclusions.

The "investigations," from the evidence we have, amounted to little more than letters, interviews, and writing papers. This is the sort of thing

---

12 Westcott, B. F. (1885), 105.

28   Chapter 2 – Prophets of a New Age?

young intellectuals with too much free time on their hands engage in regularly, but there is absolutely no evidence of their involvement in seances or forms of necromancy as Riplinger claims. Obviously, within such a group, some might go on to become more involved than others but Westcott disassociated himself from their endeavors as he concluded such investigations "led to no good."[13] Thus a fling of faddish inquiry while young followed by a later act of discernment becomes, under Riplinger's distorted lens, the making of an occult practitioner.

The other club Riplinger mentions is the Hermes Club. So what was the Hermes Club? It turns out it was a group of young classical scholars who would get together and read papers they had written and receive input by others in the group. The name was chosen because the Greek god Hermes was associated with literature and the arts. The subjects of the papers Westcott contributed were as follows:

> The Lydian Origin of the Etruscans; The Nominative Absolute; The Roman Games of (or at) Ball; The so-called Aoristic Use of the Perfect in Latin; The Funeral Ceremonies of the Romans; The Eleatic School of Philosophy; The Mythology of the Homeric Poems; The Theology of Aristotle; Theramenes.[14]

It is difficult to imagine much of that leading to satanic rituals.

So where does Riplinger get her ideas that this was an occult organization? Much of it stems from her lack of knowledge compounded by her reliance on discredited sources such as Madame Blavatksy and Barbara G. Walker. She concludes Hermes is Satan because his name is associated with various occult ideas and organizations (e.g., The Hermetic Order of the Golden Dawn) that stem from an ancient movement, revived in the Renaissance, known as Hermetism.

What she does not understand is the Hermes of such movements is not

---

13 Westcott, A. (1903a), 119.
14 Westcott, A. (1903a), 47.

Chapter 2 – Prophets of a New Age?

the Greek god Hermes for whom the Hermes Club was named but the supposed sage/god Hermes Trismegistus. The latter stems from the late period of Hellenistic Egypt and was based on the Egyptian god Thoth. Thus even this "connection" to the occult – a purely nominative one – is without merit.

The final accusation of the three is to place Westcott in a line of occult leaders as one who "took the wand and relayed it into the twentieth century."[15] Yet, when one looks at the footnote for this assertion, it is built on the baseless identification of Brooke Foss Westcott with the noted occultist William Wynn Westcott. She bases her conjecture on the following items:

1. Articles in Blavatsky *Theosophical Dictionary* were contributed at the special request of Blavatsky by Brother W. W. Westcott.
2. B. F. Westcott is mentioned elsewhere in her books.
3. Westcott's son mentioned his the "B" opening his father's signature was often mistaken for a "W."
4. W. W. Westcott is the name given as founder of the Hermetic Order of the Golden Dawn.
5. W. W. Westcott wrote a book on the Pymander of Hermes.
6. B. F. Westcott was involved with the Hermes Club.[16]

She then just assumes B. F. Westcott and W. W. Westcott were one and the same before adding it was all speculation on her part. Well, if it is speculation, then is not the statement that Westcott was an occultist passing on the wand speculation as well? That someone's name should not be tarnished by such dishonesty normally would not require explanation.

Even a minimum amount of research combined with some common sense would debunk the absurd reasoning above. If Blavatksy thought enough of someone to include papers by them and consider them a

---
15 *NABV*, 425.
16 *NABV*, 676-677.

30   Chapter 2 – Prophets of a New Age?

"brother" in her cause, she would certainly be aware of his name and not have referred to him as "W. W. Westcott." The fact that Blavatsky mentions B. F. Westcott elsewhere indicates she knows the difference between them. As for the implications of her mentioning his name, Blavatsky tried to present her society's work as "scholarly" and often quoted the intelligentsia of her day and usually distorted what they had written in the process. Westcott was one of these sources and he had no control over her pen. Finally, as mentioned earlier, Riplinger clearly does not understand the Hermes Trismegistus of Hermetism (the Pymander is a Hermetic document) and the Greek Hermes taken as a name by the Hermes Club were not the same mythological figure.

Even worse, the Westcott who contributed papers to the Theosophical Society is clearly identified as W. Wynn Westcott in the same book Riplinger cited. In fact, Dr. William Wynn Westcott was a known occultist, the founder of the Hermetic Society of the Golden Dawn, and a member of the Theosophical Society. He is not the same person as Brooke Foss Westcott and they are not even relatives. They are merely two people with the same last name. This is apparently enough of a connection to declare someone as occultist in the mind of Gail Riplinger.

Riplinger continues to drive home this fallacious claim by manipulating quotes from Westcott to match that of Blavatsky. At one point she has them both stating "There is one life … "[17] but, of course, when the source is checked, the context is completely different. Blavatsky is making some monist pronouncement on existence while Westcott is speaking of the unity of the Body of Christ in the Communion of Saints referred to in the Apostles' Creed. In referring to the life of Christ we now share as His disciples in communion with Him, Westcott writes:

> The communion of saints in the largest sense, the communion of angels and men, of men already perfected, and of men struggling towards the crown which is prepared for them, is a present reality. There is one divine kingdom,

---
17 *NABV*, 412.

> and there are many worlds. **There is one life** which finds expression in many forms, but that life is greater, deeper than all.[18]

This distortion clearly mangles the context by equating Blavatsky's monism with Westcott's description of unity in the Communion of Saints.

Riplinger follows this distortion by comparing a fuller version of the same quote by Blavatsky ("There is one life eternal invisible") to three quotes by Westcott:

> There is one life which has expressions in many forms
>
> … the one life if fulfilled in many parts …
>
> To make of life one harmonious whole, to realize the invisible.[19]

Given Riplinger's dismal track record thus far, her testimony should hardly be accepted at face value.

The first quote is a misstatement of a larger portion of the earlier quote "There is one life" by Westcott. Riplinger quotes him stating "There is one life which has expression in many forms", inferring some type of monism, while Westcott, as we can see previously, actually wrote "There is one life which *finds* expression in many forms..." and is addressing how the life of Christ finds expression through his disciples in this life and the life to come.

The second quote is yet another attempt to use an isolated phrase to point to ontological monism, but instead Westcott is addressing the interconnectedness of our lives, our responsibilities to each other, and how such an awareness allows us to resist the evils arising from selfishness:

> And it is obvious that this belief in the solidarity of life, if once we could give it vivid distinctness, is able—perhaps is alone able—to deal with the evils which spring from

---

18 Westcott, B. F. (1885), 249.
19 *NABV*, 413.

32   Chapter 2 – Prophets of a New Age?

> selfishness. It enables us to estimate rightly the burden of poverty and the heavier burden of wealth, when we take account of the conditions under which **the one life is fulfilled in many parts**. It quickens that keen sense of responsibility to God which best regulates the use of large means; and it quickens that conviction of Divine fellowship which brings dignity even to indigence. And meanwhile it delivers us from the bondage of material standards, when it makes known all that is of the earth as that through which the spiritual is brought within our reach.[20]

How this has anything to do with the occult or New Age is known only to Gail Riplinger and her devoted followers.

The final quote is perhaps the most absurd of all. She notes a saying Westcott often used but spends no effort determining its original context or the author's intent. Instead she just assumes "Westcott is an occultist" and runs with it. When we place this in its original context, a sermon following the death of a beloved cathedral organist of thirty years, her claims once again are exposed as bogus:

> To repeat then what has been said, the belief in the Resurrection of Christ harmonizes life, inspires life, transforms life. The words are lofty words, and if for us they are words only they bear with them the sad condemnation of a noble ideal recognized and abandoned. But, my friends, I cannot think that we shall rest contented with the possibility of such an issue. **To make of life one harmonious whole, to realize the invisible**, to anticipate the transfiguring majesty of the Divine Presence, is all that is worth living for. What life is, as we see its outward form in the vain shadow of earth, the lesson of the last two days may teach us. Suddenly, without time for special preparation or parting counsel, one of our own body passed

---

20 Westcott, B. F. (1891a), 357.

Chapter 2 – Prophets of a New Age?

almost at once from the fulfillment of his daily ministry to helpless unconsciousness, from unconsciousness to his final rest ; but by a most touching coincidence the last words which he accompanied in this Cathedral express, as we trust, his last prayer and his last confession, and breathe comfort beyond any words of man : *Lo! this is our GOD, we have waited for Him, and He will save us : this is the LORD, we have waited for Him, we will be glad and rejoice in His salvation.* I cannot, as a stranger, speak with fit judgment of his services, but I know that they were long, that they were faithful, that they were zealous ; and I know that work so done by the grace of GOD, follows him who has been enabled to do it, to bear fruit beyond all that we can imagine, and that the memory of it survives to be a silent power for good among those who shall come after. Death, after earthly duty loyally, humbly, patiently fulfilled, is not the end but the beginning of life. That is the Gospel of the Resurrection to which our thoughts have been turned this morning; and may GOD in His great mercy grant to us all to know, as our hope is our brother knew, not in word but in power, the Gospel which we preach and ye believed, the Gospel of Christ's Passion and Christ's Triumph.[21]

Are we to believe that Christians anticipating Christ's transfiguring majesty are harbingers of the occult?

Unwilling to stop here with her spurious claims, "Gail the Ripper" then goes on a discourse intermingling a quote from Westcott with those of various occult sources and ties them together as through they were dealing with the same subject. Of course, to do this, she needs to once again carefully screen his words so no one will recognize he is speaking on an unrelated topic. She uses the following "quote" to hammer home her unsupported monistic theme:

---

21 Westcott, B. F. (1869).

34   Chapter 2 – Prophets of a New Age?

> [T]he connection by which we are bound one to another ... is found to be more powerful and more far-reaching. It is the element – one element – in the idea of life which has been specifically revealed to us in this age.[22]

Not surprisingly, the quote has an entirely different context. Here he is speaking of a social connection between all of mankind and our responsibilities to each other and not an ontological connection arising from some sort of New Age idea monism:

> There can be no doubt that the uniform tendency of recent research is to establish in many unexpected ways the closeness of **the connexion by which we are bound one to another**. In proportion as we know more fully, this connexion **is found to be more powerful and more far-reaching. It is the element—one element—in the idea of life which has been specially revealed to us in this age**. We may conclude therefore that it is designed by the Providence of God for our special use. And it is distinctly recognised in the New Testament. We can now perceive at length that the phrases which describe the dependence of man upon man, and the mutual relations of man and nature, and the divine purpose of uniting all things 'in Christ,' are to be taken literally. They shew us that the divine revelation of life is the revelation of that larger life which we can painfully and dimly see to be now. We have in them the promise, the prophecy, of a life in which there is the unity of infinite peace and the energy of infinite love, the peace of God and the love of God, ' we in Him and He in us.'[23]

Thus, once again, the context reveals the distortions.

Riplinger is no better in her assaults upon Hort. Early in *NABV*, she ties him to a New Age plot merely because he used the word "one" in the

---

22 *NABV*, 413.
23 Westcott, B. F. (1885), 147-148.

Chapter 2 – Prophets of a New Age?

phrase "One who is the Creator."[24] She absurdly identifies any use of the term "one" by an opponent with a New Age deity regardless of its context. In this case, the context shows Hort pointing out how the conflict with the Gnostic heretics in the early centuries of the Church clarified the issues at hand for the early Christians and, specifically, how it affirmed in their mind the truth that Jesus Christ was truly God in the flesh:

> While on the subject I may as well call your attention to a suggestive note of Dorner's (you will find it by the word ' Sonntag' in the index: mine is the second edition), which I was looking at the other day; it illustrates much that you say, and connects the Sabbath with a thought that has often occurred to me, how important is the view which the conflict with gnosticism led the early Fathers to take of our Lord's life and ministry, as especially the work of **One who *was* the Creator**.[25]

The "One" in this case is clearly Jesus Christ. Thus Gail Riplinger had declared an affirmation of the divinity of Jesus to be a New Age belief.

Riplinger also points to Hort being a member of a group that became known as "the Apostles" and infers its purposes were connected to the occult. As reasons she points to its exclusive membership and its secrecy concerning discussions at their meetings. In her mind, it is the typical "secret society" such as makes the rounds among many conspiracy theorists. Noting the following passage in the biography of Hort (by his son), she infers sinister motives by the group:

> [I]n June [he] joined the mysterious company of the Apostles ... [H]e was mainly responsible for the oath which binds the members to a conspiracy of silence.[26]

She then combines this with a supposed admission of the questionable character of the "Apostles" when Hort wrote to the Rev. John Ellenton:

---
24 *NABV*, 89.
25 Hort, A. F. (1896), 246.
26 *NABV*, 415.

36   Chapter 2 – Prophets of a New Age?

> I fear you scarcely tolerate my having joined "the Apostles."[27]

So what was the nature of this group? In fact, it is quite clear the intention was to have leading young intellectuals meet in an environment where they could freely share ideas without having a cloud of suspicion hanging over their heads. It was the nineteenth century version of what we would now call a "think tank" but the price of free intellectual exchanges in Victorian England could be the loss of one's reputation and livelihood. This group allowed these men to share their ideas without such fears. In fact, its nature is quite clear when the passage is placed in context with the types of papers Hort contributed:

> Yet he found time to attend the meetings of various societies, and **in June joined the mysterious company of the "Apostles."** The first paper which he contributed was on the subject "Might is Right", in defence of Carlyle. The titles of other papers read by him were: "Can Pope teach our young poets to sing?" (a criticism of a *dictum* of C. Kingsley); "Is government an evil?" (a defence of authority); "Must the giants live apart?" (on a saying of Thackeray); "Is irony less true than matter of fact?"; "Is wealth the foundation of rank?"; "Should all honours be given to the horrible?"; "Can anything be proved by Logic?". Most of these were not so much essays as challenges to discussion, couched in a paradoxical form. He remained always a grateful and loyal member of the secret Club, which has now become famous for the number of distinguished men who have belonged to it. In his time the Club was in a manner reinvigorated, and **he was mainly responsible for the wording of the oath which binds the members to a conspiracy of silence.** Mr. Vernon Lushington remembers that at the Apostles' meetings he considered Hort "the most remarkable figure of our time,"

---

27 *NABV*, 415

Chapter 2 – Prophets of a New Age?

and that he " always spoke very seriously on these occasions."[28]

As for the alleged admission in his letter to Rev. Ellenton, in context Hort is clearly being jovial and making light of the supposed seriousness of their discussions:

> **I fear you scarcely tolerate my having joined the 'Apostles,'** but you must not judge too much by vague impressions. The record book of proceedings is very amusing; think of Maurice voting that virtue in women proceeds more from fear than modesty! It is a good sign that there is always a large number of neutral votes. Some of _____'s are ludicrous enough; *e.g.* on the question whether we ought to follow the text of Scripture or the discoveries of science as to the formation of the earth, etc. He votes the latter, adding a note that he considers the question of very little consequence, as he 'does not believe in matter'![29]

The Cambridge Apostles still exist and have had many prestigious (and some notorious) members over their existence. Things have been very much what you would expect of any such group at one of the worlds' premier institutions of higher learning.

Perhaps to prove there are no lows to which she is incapable of sinking, Riplinger even attempts to twist the words of Hort's own mother against him. She portrays a rift between the two by taking the following passage from the aforementioned biography:

> Her religious feelings were deep and strong ... [H]is mother was ... an adherent of the Evangelical school and she was to a certain degree hampered by it ... She was unable to enter into his theological views which to her

---

28 Hort, A. F. (1896), 170-171.
29 Hort, A. F. (1896), 198.

38   Chapter 2 – Prophets of a New Age?

> generation seemed a desertion of the ancient way; thus pathetically enough, there came to be a barrier between mother and son. The close intercourse on subjects which lay nearest to the hearts of each was broken ... [Concerning] her different point of view, ... he ... had to recognize that the point of view *was* different. She studied and know her bible well.[30]

Riplinger infers from the above that the split between the two were on matters that imperiled Hort's very soul. She imagines Hort's mother was an Evangelical Christian much like herself and asserts his mother wrote a letter pleading with him so he would not be missing from the righteous at the end of days:

> ... the many mansions of our Heavenly Father's House and my darling, How happy it will be if we all meet there; no one missing of all our household.[31]

Thus, if one were to believe Gail Riplinger's portrayal of the relationship between Hort and his mother, the latter fretted over the possibility her son was hellbound.

As with Riplinger's other accusations, there is far less there than meets the eye. First of all, the disagreement between Hort and his mother concerned theological disputes raging at the time within the Church of England. Hort's mother was of the "low church" (Evangelical) party while Hort had sided with the "high church" (Catholic) party then in the ascendancy through the influence of the Oxford Movement. As anyone familiar with Anglicanism would know, the terms "Evangelical" and "Catholic" have an entirely different meaning in that setting than in the larger church. An Evangelical in the Church of England would strike most modern Evangelicals as decidedly Catholic by their standards. Riplinger is apparently ignorant of such points of ecclesiology.

---

30 *NABV*, 627.
31 *NABV*, 627.

Chapter 2 – Prophets of a New Age?

Once placed back in its original context, Riplinger's mishandling of the passage becomes quite clear:

> The mother, who, unconsciously perhaps, was the real controlling force of the household, was a woman of great mental power, which she brought to bear on every detail of daily life. She had been extremely well educated, so far as the opportunities of that day allowed ; in English especially her training had been sound, and she could always express herself easily and gracefully ; both in writing and in speaking she used words in the most exact manner. Her education had given her the thoroughness and scrupulous accuracy which she transmitted to her son. She grasped firmly whatever she took in hand and mastered any book which she read. Her reading was not wide, but she was interested in current literature of the more serious sort, such as biographies and books of travel. **Her religious feelings were deep and strong.** *Circumstances had made her* **an adherent of the Evangelical school, and she was to a certain degree hampered by it**; the Oxford Movement filled her with dread and anxiety as to its possible effect on her son. **She was unable to enter into his theological views, which to her school and generation seemed a desertion of the ancient ways; thus, pathetically enough, there came to be a barrier between mother and son. The close intercourse on subjects which lay nearest to the hearts of each was broken**, to the loss and sorrow of both. His love and veneration for his mother remained unimpaired, and his letters to her show his delicate *consideration* **for her different point of view**; but it is sad that **he** should have **had to recognise that the point of view** *was* **different. She studied and knew her Bible well,** and her own religious life was most carefully regulated.[32]

---

32 Hort, A. F. (1896), 7-8.

40   Chapter 2 – Prophets of a New Age?

Hence, the disagreement between the two concerned the differences between Evangelical and Oxford Movement Anglicanism and not an issue that imperiled the soul.

While the mistake above may be understood as stemming from Riplinger's theological ignorance, the supposed quote from the "pleading letter" is an example of "Gail the Ripper" at her most dishonest. First of all, the letter in context displays no concern for anyone's eternal security. It was actually looking forward to the day the family would be reunited in eternal bliss:

> The outside of the house at Haveningham is so completely altered, I should not have known it for my dear old home. I have not seen the inside, for Mrs. Owen is too unwell to admit visitors; I should like to see it. We must think often of **the many mansions of our Heavenly Father's House, and, my darling, how happy it will be if we all meet there ; not one missing, of all our household** here; then we shall care no more what home we had in this world, than we care now what sort of cradle we were rocked in.— So let us all press forward !33

The letter is thus actually a word of encouragement for her son to continue pressing forward in his faith so they all might meet on the other side. But, just when you think the deception could not possibly get any worse, it does. For the greeting of the letter states "My dearest Arthur." Thus, this letter is not addressed to F. J. A. Hort at all but to his brother Arthur! In fact, just so the point would not be missed, the source referenced by Riplinger labels it "To Arthur Josiah Hort from his Mother" in large centered print.[34]

Whatever one may think of Westcott and Hort, their Greek text, and their theology, there is absolutely no excuse for the distortions of their work by Gail Riplinger. Not only does she manipulate their writings to

---
33 Hort, A. F. (1896), 15.
34 Hort, A. F. (1896), 15.

Chapter 2 – Prophets of a New Age?

force upon them ideas they never conceived, but in cases where her quotes are reasonably accurate, she fails to grasp the ideas being conveyed. As with Edwin H. Palmer, Westcott and Hort were intellectuals whose writings often sail completely over Gail Riplinger's rather pedestrian understanding of theology. Having no grasp of the concepts being discussed, she, out of pure ignorance, chooses to supply villainous intent as their motive.

Having now seen how she distorts the words of other Christians with whom she disagrees, we next will turn to her handling of the Word of God. As might be expected, her accuracy with the Holy Scriptures fares no better.

Chapter 3 – Errors of Biblical Proportions

The errors noted in the previous chapter are quite shocking but Gail Riplinger is often no more careful handling the text of Holy Scripture than the words of Biblical scholars. Verses in modern translations differing from the rendering in the King James Version are attributed to "New Age" ideas and the changes themselves are sometimes completely fabricated. If she handles the Word of God without the slightest concern for honesty and integrity, then why should Christians take her seriously elsewhere?

An interesting example occurs early in the first chapter of NABV when Riplinger asserts modern translations are intended to prepare us for the worship of the antichrist by changing key verses. Providing an example in the modern renderings of Philippians 3:3, she claims "worship God" from the KJV has been replaced with "worship" in modern versions.[1] The inference is the modern translations (NIV, NASB, et al.) have removed the reference to God to prepare us to worship … who knows what? Such a change might strike Christians as alarming but is it accurate?

When one checks modern translations of the verse, it is clear Riplinger has played fast and loose with the facts. The change is not "worship God" to "worship" but "worship God in the spirit" (KJV) to either "worship in the Spirit of God" (NIV, ESV) or "worship by the Spirit of God" (NASB). Now, whatever opinion one holds on the proper rendering of this verse, the accusation the modern translations have removed the mention of God is false. Furthermore, the inference that worshipping "in the Spirit of God" leads to the worship of the antichrist is an absurdity that demonstrates

---

[1] *NABV*, 9.

44   Chapter 3 – Errors of Biblical Proportions

once more Riplinger's dishonesty in handling the evidence.

Similar misrepresentations are on display when Riplinger approaches the question of personal pronouns in the text. There are cases where the KJV uses "Jesus" or "God" while modern translations use "he" or "him." Riplinger suggests this might be preparing us for the great deception to come.[2] But is there any substance behind her wild accusations?

When one examines the context of the passages she cites, the "he" referred to is clearly the same as in the KJV. The study of the Greek manuscripts has led scholars to believe the pronouns were at some point changed to the more explicit name. The most likely reason was for the purposes of reading texts in the Church. Christians of the early centuries most commonly came in contact with Holy Scripture in the Church's worship. If a reading for a specific week began using a pronoun, it might be unclear who the pronoun referred to and so the pronoun was changed to the more explicit form to clarify the issue.

A case in point can be seen in the very first text Riplinger cites: Luke 24:36.[3] The passage is a segue between the earlier passage of the disciples on the road to Emmaus and Jesus appearing to the Apostles in the Upper Room. Throughout the earlier passage, Jesus is referred to many times by pronouns in both modern versions and the KJV. So why are these other references not leading us to the New Age but only the one that follows? The reference to Jesus by a pronoun is no less obvious in Luke 24:36 than the verses that preceded it. Even worse, Riplinger is again dishonest in her presentation as modern versions such as the NIV, ESV, and NJKV do use the name "Jesus" in this verse rather than the pronoun. Thus, not only is Riplinger's conclusion false, but also her premise.

A related piece of nonsense arises when Riplinger points to the use of neutral pronouns such as "the one." She attempts to tie this in with an androgynous "New Age" deity but nothing of the sort is intended. The reality is contemporary English no longer uses the masculine to identify an

---
2   *NABV*, 17.
3   *NABV*, 17.

Chapter 3 – Errors of Biblical Proportions   45

unspecified person of either sex. Thus, what appeared as "he" in the KJV will often be rendered "the one" in newer translations. This has nothing to do with the Greek but supplies the proper rendering for the present state of the language.

There are certainly cases where some translations may be accused of "political correctness" by using the neutral rendering where a male is specifically denoted and criticism in these cases is justified. However, these generally appear in versions such as the NRSV favored by "mainline denominations" and not those commonly used by Evangelicals. It also has more to do with "political correctness" run amok than anything to do with the occult. We may argue over the proper boundaries for "gender neutral" language but to claim this indicates some quasi-occultic deity is absurd. Yet Riplinger insists on connecting such renderings to the occult by bizarre applications of free word association.

As insane as these sorts of wild assertions might be, it is strained further when Riplinger's own ignorance of the ancient languages compounds the error. An example is her description of the differences between modern translations and the KJV in rendering Isaiah 14:12. Where the KJV reads "Lucifer," most modern translations will have something along the lines of "morning star" or "daystar" with the newer renderings being the proper translation of the Hebrew "heylel." Riplinger disputes this by noting the latter does not contain the Hebrew for "star" and thus demonstrates she has no grasp of the subject. After all, "Sirius" is our name for the dog star but it also does not contain the word "star." The Hebrew "heylel" was used for the morning star as was the Latin word "lucifer" but neither had any background as a proper name.

Much of the confusion arose through interpretations of the verse as referring to Satan. Many Christians believed it referred to the casting down of Satan and so lucifer, the Latin translation of heylel, became synonymous with Satan. Some even claimed it was Satan's name prior to his being cast out of heaven but how he would have garnered a name in the Latin language was left unexplained.

46   Chapter 3 – Errors of Biblical Proportions

I will leave the question of whether the verse refers to Satan open since there are sincere Christians who hold differing views on the interpretation of this verse. But there is no reason to insist a Latin word be transliterated into English as a proper name.

An attempt at a slam dunk by pointing to Jesus being referred to as "morning star" in the New Testament is also a failure. Any careful exegesis of the passages shows the term is used quite differently in each. In Isaiah 14:12, the term "morning star" is obviously used mockingly as someone who sought to rise to the position of the most high. The self-proclaimed "morning star" described in the verse was a pretender and a fraud and not the true star at all. Jesus, on the other hand, is given the title in praise as he is the true "Morning Star." Thus, even if one were to accept Riplinger's premises concerning the passage, her conclusion is a non sequitur.

More silliness occurs when she accuses modern translations of intentionally omitting the word "dragon" from Biblical passages to hide the role of Satan. There are 34 verses where the word "dragon" occurs in the KJV. The twelve in the New Testament all occur in the Book of Revelation and all are clearly used as symbols of Satan. These twelve remain in the ESV, NASB, and NIV. The Old Testament verses usually are not referring to Satan but rather to some actual earthly creature. In these cases it is quite ridiculous to translate the reference as "dragon."

Moreover, even in the case where the reference is pointing to eschatological concerns (i.e., Isaiah 27:1), there is no necessity for the translation to be rendered "dragon" since Satan is referred to by other terms in the Scriptures. For example, the term "serpent" is also used and this is a much more obvious reference than "dragon" since the story of the Garden of Eden is better known among Christians. Could not those who use modern translations accuse the KJV translators of hiding the reference to the serpent by using a less obvious term? The point is that this sort of argument is clearly circular: Riplinger does not argue from the Hebrew text but merely assumes the KJV is correct and argues the others must then

Chapter 3 – Errors of Biblical Proportions 47

be wrong because they differ from the KJV.

This can be seen clearly in her inconsistent methodology. If the KJV rendering agrees with the Majority Text, she will point to the many thousands of copies supporting it (never mentioning that this vast majority arises from manuscripts from the tenth century or later) but when the KJV differs from the Majority Text this supposedly determining factor is ignored. There is no consistent approach to defending the KJV text because there is no standard apart from merely assuming a priori the KJV is correct in all its readings.

If all else fails in her defense of the KJV, Riplinger merely distorts the modern renderings. She will focus on a particular verse in a particular translation and imply it is representative of all modern versions. The examples given are often from such paraphrases as *The Living Bible* that are not at all consistent with other modern translations and usually include theological biases in their renderings. Any translation of the Bible contains some renderings that can be called into question. If one wants to uphold a particular version as the one true Bible, it is easy to pick out the possible errors in *all other* versions and project the view that *each* is representative of *all*. We could then have an NASB-only movement or an ESV-only movement that would be equally silly.

Perhaps the bottom of Riplinger's barrel of tricks is misrepresenting the actual renderings of the newer versions for the sole purpose of finding fault where none exists. The distortion of Philippians 3:3 mentioned earlier is an example of this but is by no means the only such example. She pulls a similar trick when dealing with Isaiah 26:3 where she compares the NASB and KJV and she cites as follows:

> The steadfast of mind Thou wilt keep in perfect peace (NASB)
>
> Thou wilt keep him in perfect peace, whose mind is stayed on thee (KJV)

Here it certainly appears that something is quite wrong with the NASB

48   Chapter 3 – Errors of Biblical Proportions

rendering as the steadfastness of mind is not explicitly defined as depending on God. However, this is not the complete rendering for either translation of this verse and Riplinger has again cut a section out to distort the intent:

> The steadfast of mind You will keep in perfect peace, Because he trusts in You. (NASB)

> Thou wilt keep *him* in perfect peace, *whose* mind *is* stayed *on thee*: because he trusteth in thee. (KJV)

Note that the NASB reference in context now does have an implicit reference to the mind being stayed on God through the later mention of "because he trusts in You." But, more importantly, note the italics of the KJV translation that the translators used to indicate words not part of the original verse but added to clarify the meaning. The very "on thee" cited by Riplinger as "omitted" was actually added by the KJV translators for clarification and was not part of the original Hebrew. Now some translators follow the KJV in such clarification but one could hardly fault the NASB translators for choosing to use a more literal rendering.

Further examples of her manipulation of Holy Scripture can be given but this short overview should provide a taste of the hysterical assertions and misrepresentations present in her handling of Bible translations. Even when handling the Bible itself, Gail Riplinger continues her pattern of dishonesty.

Chapter 4 – The Catholic Menace

When King James Onlyists such as Gail Riplinger attack modern translations, a commonly used tactic is "guilt by association." Riplinger knows her core audience is among fundamentalist who are often united in their opposition to Roman Catholicism. Thus, if you portray the newer versions as somehow infected with the "errors of Rome," this proves they are corrupt and, hence, the KJV is the "one true Bible."

The fact this line of reasoning is a complete non sequitur never dawns on those using it. After all, even if modern translations were "papal plots," this does not prove anything about the KJV. Who's to say the KJV doesn't have the same problem and the Geneva Bible isn't the "one true Bible"? Little in the way of evidence supporting such claims is forthcoming and the result is merely the rambling of a conspiracy theorist.

Attempts to paint modern translations as tainted by Catholicism are certainly not unique to Riplinger in the world of King James Onlyism. One commonly used claim asserts manuscripts used in modern critical editions of the Greek New Testament (e.g., Codex Sinaiticus and Codex Vaticanus) have the Greek Septuagint, including the Apocrypha accepted by Catholics and not Protestants, as their Old Testament. This supposedly demonstrates "Roman leanings." However, what they do not tell you is the Byzantine codices underlying the KJV also contained the Septuagint as their Old Testament.

Another tactic is to accuse the editors of modern translations with "sacramentalism." This is the idea grace of God is communicated through the sacraments of Baptism and the Lord's Supper (Eucharist) rather than

Chapter 4 – The Catholic Menace

viewing the latter as mere symbols. The backers of King James Onlyism are most often fundamentalist Baptists who reject the sacraments as means of real grace and consider this a sign of "Roman corruption."

In making such assertions, King James Onlyists displays their complete ignorance of the theology of the King James translators. These men were members of the Church of England whose understanding of the faith was very different from most contemporary supporters of their translation. The KJV translators were, for the most part, Anglican clergy who worshipped under the Book of Common Prayer and were required to uphold the 39 Articles of Religion as outlining the essentials of Christian orthodoxy. These two documents set forth the liturgical and sacramental nature of the Church of England.

Anglicans do not share the outlook of King James Onlyists but have historically seen themselves as "Reformed Catholics" charting a "via media" between Rome and Protestantism. For example, the following beliefs, all just as "Catholic" if not more so than anything associated with the creators of modern translations, appear in the 39 Articles of Religion upheld by the vast majority of KJV translators:

1. While the books of the Apocrypha are not to be considered canonical, they are held in high esteem and read by the Church for example of life and instruction of manners but not to establish doctrine (Article VI). The original 1611 KJV contained the Apocrypha between the Old and New Testaments and references were given in the notes for the Old and New Testaments to these books.

2. The Nicene, Apostles', and Athanasian Creeds are to be received and believed as provable from Holy Scripture (Article VIII).

3. The Son of God was eternally begotten of the Father (implicitly through the Nicene Creed and explicitly in Article II). This is a point where, as we shall later see, Gail Riplinger proves herself completely ignorant of historic Christian doctrine believed by the

Chapter 4 – The Catholic Menace

KJV translators themselves.

4. After Christ died for us and was buried, he descended into Hell (implicitly through the Apostles' Creed and explicitly in Article III).

5. The Church accept the doctrine of original sin (Article IX).

6. The Church has the power to decree Rites and Ceremonies not explicitly mentioned in Scripture so long as they do not contradict Scripture (Article XX).

7. Public preaching and administration of the Sacraments of the Church are only legitimately executed by those men called and sent by a congregation (Article XXIII).

8. Sacraments are not mere tokens of our professions of faith but are sure witnesses and signs of effectual grace by which God works invisibly in us and strengthens and confirms our faith (Article XXV).

9. Baptism is not merely an outward sign of our profession of faith but is a sign of our regeneration whereby those baptized are grafted into the Church, the promises of the forgiveness of sins and our adoption as sons of God by the Holy Spirit are signed and sealed, and faith confirmed and grace increased by virtue of prayer unto God (Article XXVII).

10. The practice of infant baptism is to be retained in the Church (Article XXVII).

11. The Sacrament of the Lord's Supper is not a mere sign of love but of our redemption whereby those who rightly, worthily, and with faith receive it partake in the Body and Blood of Christ (Article XXVIII).

12. While rejecting transubstantiation, the Church holds the Body and Blood of Christ are received in a heavenly and spiritual manner through faith while those without faith eat and drink condemnation

Chapter 4 – The Catholic Menace

(Articles XXVIII, XXIX).

13. Bishops, priests, and deacons are rightly consecrated and ordered according to the practice set forth by the Church (Article XXXVI).

If such beliefs were agreed upon by scholars working on modern translations, one could imagine the outcry from the KJV Only camp. Yet here these quite sacramental beliefs are agreed upon by the KJV translators and is completely overlooked.

Further evidence of the "Reformed Catholicism" of the KJV translators occurs in the Book of Common Prayer setting forth the worship of the Church of England. As Anglican clergy, they led the people in these prayers regularly. One of the best known is the Prayer of Humble Access recited before Communion:

> We do not presume to come to this thy Table (O merciful Lord) trusting in our own righteousness, but in thy manifold and great mercies. We be not worthy so much as to gather up the crumbs under thy Table. But thou art the same Lord, whose property is always to have mercy: Grant us therefore, gracious Lord, so to eat the Flesh of thy dear Son Jesus Christ, and to drink his Blood, in these holy Mysteries, that we may continually dwell in him, and he in us, that our sinful bodies may be made clean by his Body, and our souls washed through his most precious Blood. Amen.

It is difficult to imagine many King James Onlyists following the translators of their "perfect Bible" in holding the Body and Blood of Christ being consumed through the "holy mysteries." Nor could one imagine most King James Onlyists signing reciting, as would have the KJV translators, this prayer prior to the baptizing of an infant:

> Almighty and everlasting God, who of thy great mercy didst save Noah and his family in the Ark, from perishing by water, and also didst safely lead the children of Israel,

Chapter 4 – The Catholic Menace 53

> thy people, through the Red Sea, figuring thereby thy holy Baptism; and by the Baptism of thy well-beloved son Jesus Christ, didst sanctify the River Jordan, and all other waters, to the mystical washing away of sin; We beseech thee (for thine infinite mercies) that thou wilt mercifully look upon these children, sanctify them and wash them with the Holy Ghost, that they being delivered from thy wrath, may be received into the Ark of Christ's Church, and being steadfast in faith, joyful through hope, and rooted in charity, may so pass the waves of this troublesome world, that finally they may come to the land of everlasting life, there to reign with thee, world without end, through Jesus Christ our Lord. Amen.

Nor is it quite imaginable most King James Onlyists would follow the KJV translators in marking the child with the sign of the cross after the baptism and stating:

> We receive this child into the congregation of Christ's
> flock, and do sign him with the sign of the cross, in token
> that hereafter he shall not be ashamed to confess the faith
> of Christ crucified, and manfully to fight under his banner
> against sin, the world, and the devil, and to continue
> Christ's faithful soldier and servant unto his lifes end.
> Amen.

Nor would the King James Only crowd approve of the following prayer of thanksgiving that would have been recited by the King James translators after they had performed a baptism in which they thank God for granting the child the gift of baptismal regeneration:

> We yield thee hearty thanks most merciful father, that it
> hath pleased thee to regenerate this infant with thy Holy
> Spirit, to receive him for thine own child by adoption, and
> to incorporate him into thy holy Church. And humbly we
> beseech thee to grant that he being dead unto sin and living

54 Chapter 4 – The Catholic Menace

> unto righteousness, and being buried with Christ in his death, may crucify the old man, and utterly abolish the whole body of sin, that as he is made partaker of the death of thy Son, so he may be partaker of His Resurrection, so that finally with the residue of thy holy Church, he may be an inheritor of thine everlasting kingdom. Through Christ our Lord. Amen.

The reality of the beliefs of the KJV translators stands in sharp contrast to those held by the vast majority of those holding the King James Only view.

Such inconvenient truths were not restricted to the normative statements of the Church of England. There is no greater enemy of King James Onlyism than the KJV translators themselves as they express their views in the preface to the 1611 KJV. Two of the supposed enemies of truth, Origen and Jerome, are singled out for praise in their handling of the Holy Scriptures in, respectively, the Hexapala and the Vulgate. This might be quite a shock to most King James Onlyists who heap scorn upon both these works but the KJV translators were of a far different opinion. This is particularly the case with Jerome, translator of the Catholic Vulgate, to whom they prefix the abbreviation for "Saint" and cite as a respected authority throughout the preface.

As for the specifics, it is stated that Origen worthily and to great purpose compiled the Hexapala and they are far more effusive in their praise of Jerome's work on the Vulgate:

> There were also within a few hundred years after Christ, translations many into the Latin tongue: for this tongue also was very fit to convey the Law and the Gospel by, because in those times very many Countries of the West, yea of the South, East and North, spake or understood Latin, being made Provinces to the Romans. But now the Latin Translations were too many to be all good, for they were infinite (Latini Interprets nullo modo numerari possunt,

> saith S. Augustine.) [S. Augustin. de doctr. Christ. lib 2 cap II]. Again they were not out of the Hebrew fountain (we speak of the Latin Translations of the Old Testament) but out of the Greek stream, therefore the Greek being not altogether clear, the Latin derived from it must needs be muddy. This moved S. Jerome a most learned father, and the best linguist without controversy, of his age, or of any that went before him, to undertake the translating of the Old Testament, out of the very fountain with that evidence of great learning, judgment, industry, and faithfulness, that he had forever bound the Church unto him, in a debt of special remembrance and thankfulness.

Thus not only was Jerome's work considered to have left the Church owing him a special debt of remembrance, but was considered to have improved greatly upon the Old Latin it replaced. This is significant since many King James Onlyists imagine the Old Latin was akin to the KJV or Byzantine text. Of course, this is an absurdity to anyone familiar with the examples we have of the Old Latin text.

The point of all of this is not merely to specify major theological differences between the KJV translators and most King James Onlyists. Rather, it is to give clear and compelling witness to the complete double standard applied by many in the KJV Only movement. If someone such as Gail Riplinger is to attack Westcott and Hort for holding views she considers "tainted by Rome," should she not apply the same standards to the King James translators? Westcott and Hort were well within the norm of Anglicanism and far closer to those of the KJV translators than is Gail Riplinger. With a proper perspective of the theological norms within Anglicanism, attacks alleging "Roman influences" on modern translations becomes very much a case of the pot calling the kettle black. Those who translated the KJV were far closer to a Catholic view in general than similar committees on popular modern translations.

In imagining Catholic influences upon modern translations, Riplinger

Chapter 4 – The Catholic Menace

calls upon the most ridiculous of anti-catholic literature. An example is the 19th century treatise *The Two Babylons* by Alexander Hislop. Hislop's book, whose abuse of source materials rivals Riplinger's own, has long been standard fare within fundamentalism but its dated style made it a trying read for some. Then Ralph Woodrow, heavily relying on Hislop's material, wrote *Babylon Mystery Religion* in a much more breezy style and his book became an instant favorite with the conspiracy theory end of fundamentalism. Later, Woodrow was challenged to check the material he had used and found, to his great shock, it was all nonsense and Hislop's own sources contradicted his claims. Woodrow, to his credit, then withdrew his book from publication and wrote a new one (*Babylon Mystery Religion?*) refuting Hislop's (and his own earlier) work. Despite this questionable lineage, Riplinger not only uses Hislop as a source but also uses Woodrow's earlier work: a book that had been disowned by its own author years before!

The supposed links to the Catholic Church are merely an attempt to avoid having to present any substantial evidence. Riplinger is aware that her core audience will often condemn anything associated with Rome on that basis alone. So long as she doesn't have to reveal the same problems exist with the KJV translators, it might even work. But once the reality of the KJV translators real beliefs are known, her histrionics are revealed as little more than ignorant posturing.

Chapter 5 – Acrostic Algebra and Revelation

Perhaps the most bizarre portion of NABV is when Gail Riplinger introduces something she calls "Acrostic Algebra." This much discussed topic, appearing at the beginning of Part 2 of the book[1], is the "adding" of the acronyms for various modern Bible translations, "subtracting" the acronym "AV" (for Authorized Version – another term for the KJV), and the answer supposedly results in "sin." All of this somehow proves the KJV is the one true Bible and modern versions are of Satan.

The first problem with her "procedure" is that it makes absolutely no sense. Let us put aside for the moment that such manipulations prove absolutely nothing but the ability to play with letters. Let us forget that this is the sort of manipulation present in various occult practices she supposedly condemns. Let us just consider the algebra.

When one examines her "deduction," there are no rules except the ones she makes up at each step to keep her argument afloat. These make no algebraic or logical sense. She just needs a letter or letters to disappear and finds a reason to make them do so. No step follows the same rules as the one before it or the one that follows. It is all just the illusion of logic where none actually exists.

Even worse, however, is the fact she pins the blame on God for the mess she has created. When questioned by KJV Only critic James White on the topic, she stated God have revealed the procedure to her. When questioned why she called the NASB the NASV in the procedure, her answer was that is what God calls it.

---
1 *NABV*, 149.

58   Chapter 5 – Acrostic Algebra and Revelation

Such claims to divine insight are not one-time events with Gail Riplinger. In describing the writing of NABV, she made the case for her personal pipeline to the Lord:

> Daily during the six years needed for this investigation, the Lord miraculously brought the needed materials and resources – much like the ravens fed Elijah. Each discovery was not the result of effort on my part, but of the directed hand of God--so much so that I hesitated to even put my name on the book. Consequently, I used G.A. Riplinger, which signifies to me, God and Riplinger – God as author and Riplinger as secretary.[2]

Thus, according to Gail Riplinger, it is God who is responsible for the amalgamation of dishonest citations and Biblical missteps present in NABV. As bad as it is for Riplinger herself to produce such drivel, that only affects her own reputation. But to blame her miserable output on the Lord is blasphemous.

The claims Gail Riplinger made above for NABV would place it in the same category as the Bible. Would Gail Riplinger suggest we add NABV to the Canon of Holy Scripture? That anyone could take seriously the work of someone who made the above statement after the obvious distortions of both the Bible and the work of other Christians already outlined is astounding. Yet there are many KJV Onlyists who, even after having been shown the evidence of her malfeasance, still believe she is telling the truth. KJV Onlyism is indeed a "strong delusion."

---

2   *The End Times and Victorious Living* (January/February 1994).

Chapter 6 – Manuscripts

The debate over the KJV and modern translations must eventually turn to questions over the manuscript traditions. The major difference between the KJV and the modern translations is their use of different manuscripts for the New Testament. The KJV translators consulted primarily a family of Greek critical editions compiled by Desiderius Erasmus, Robert Estienne (Stephanus), and Theodore Beza and commonly known as the Textus Receptus. Modern translations usually consult the editions of the United Bible Society (UBS) or Nestle/Aland.

The difference between these Greek critical editions are in the manuscripts used to compile them. There were very few manuscripts available to the editors of the editions of the Textus Receptus and these were generally very late and of inferior quality when compared to the manuscript tradition as a whole. Those underlying more recent editions take the whole corpus of manuscripts into consideration and attempt to arrive at the most likely early reading.

KJV Onlyists, including Gail Riplinger, have a very distorted picture of this tradition. Part of this stems from their adherence to conspiracy theories but also playing a role is that, in searching for evidence, they have turned to sources very early in the process of examining the manuscript tradition. These early battles pitted Westcott and Hort against John William Burgon, Dean of Chichester Cathedral, who supported the Textus Receptus as the basis for the New Testament. The problem is they treat the state of the argument today as though it were the same as in the nineteenth century. Yet much of the discussion, while still using the same terms, often has a very different meaning and hence discussions using these same terms from over a century ago are irrelevant to any examination of the evidence today.

Chapter 6 – Manuscripts

For example, the nineteenth century discussion would have used the term "Alexandrian reading" to refer to those appearing in either Codex Sinaiticus or Codex Vaticanus. Westcott and Hort depended almost exclusively upon those two manuscripts for their text. While these manuscripts are certainly important, scholars today would not rely upon them to the exclusion of all others. Much of the adjustment has been due to the discovery of earlier manuscripts in the twentieth century that have shown Sinaiticus and Vaticanus to themselves to be part of an evolution of the text.

The problem is many KJV Onlyists still think Westcott and Hort are used today and still think "Alexandrian" means the same thing today than it did then. As earlier manuscripts have been discovered, readings that were once considered exclusively Byzantine were also shown to occur in Alexandrian texts and neither tradition was static. That is, earlier Alexandrian texts differed from later ones just as earlier Byzantine texts differed from later ones.

There is also the issue of the KJV supposedly representing the "Majority Text." KJV Onlyists will point to the thousands of manuscripts they claim support the KJV against the far fewer supporting modern translations. This line of argumentation fails at multiple levels. First of all, the number of manuscripts is quite irrelevant to determining the state of the original text. Well over ninety percent of the extant manuscripts are from the tenth century A.D. and later. We should not determine the original text by its state in the second millennium A.D. but by its early state. There are readings in the KJV that do not occur in any Greek manuscript until well into the second millennium A.D. Should we consider these proper readings? These are obviously later alterations that were not part of the original text.

Also never considered is the use of Greek determined the state of the later manuscripts. In the early centuries of Christianity, Greek was a universal language throughout the Mediterranean world. By the fourth century A.D., Latin had taken over in the West. By the end of the first

Chapter 6 – Manuscripts

millennium, the Arab conquests had reduced Greek to the regions still under control of Constantinople. Thus the Greek New Testament became centralized under Byzantine control and their readings became dominant from the tenth century onward. It was socio-political and not textual conditions that made the Byzantine the Majority Text. Until that point, it was a minority of Greek manuscripts.

Also overlooked is that the Textus Receptus, while it is derived from the Majority Text tradition, is not itself the Majority Text. In fact, it differs from it in over 1,500 places. In fact, there are places where the Majority Text and the newer critical texts agree but the Textus Receptus (and KJV) has a different reading.

This latter point demonstrates the double standards of KJV Onlyists. There is no real methodology or standard applied except the insistence the KJV is perfect. When the KJV agrees with the Majority Text against the modern translations, this is argued as decisive evidence. However, on occasions when the reverse is true, it is overlooked. Their position has less to do with agreeing with the Majority Text than agreeing with the KJV. Thus, it is a circular argument: the KJV is assumed correct and other translations are wrong because they differ from the KJV.

In places where Riplinger attempts to address the manuscript evidence, she makes the same mistakes noted above. She relies on outdated evidence from the nineteenth century or other KJV Onlyists dependent upon them. She confuses the "Alexandrian readings" with only those present in Codex Sinaiticus or Codex Vaticanus. She uses the "Majority Text argument. Her sheer ignorance of the textual evidence is largely fed by her dependence upon outdated sources and KJV Onlyist propaganda.

Let us be clear on this point: when it comes to understanding the New Testament manuscript tradition, Gail Riplinger is clueless. She is merely repeating the errors of KJV Onlyism that have been addressed numerous times by numerous authors.[1] While some scholars have argued against the

---

1   See White (2009) and Carson (1978) for textual critiques of the KJV Onlyist position.

Chapter 6 – Manuscripts

newer critical texts and for the Majority Text in a constructive fashion[2], the KJV Onlyist view is an intellectual backwater whose adherents are largely made up of conspiracy theorists without any serious historical perspective on the textual preservation of the New Testament.

---

[2] Among scholars of the last few decades, Arthur Farstad and Maurice A. Robinson were among the most vocal supporters of the Majority Text tradition. However, both were critical of the KJV Only Movement.

Chapter 7 – Conclusion

This little booklet has merely touched the surface of the sorts of errors one finds in Gail Riplinger's *New Age Bible Versions*. Given her original work was close to 700 pages, a point-by-point refutation might take 1000 pages or more. Frankly, Riplinger's book is hardly worth such an effort but certain things did need to be addressed.

It has effectively been demonstrated that Gail Riplinger's handling of textual data is blatantly dishonest. She takes words from different sections of a book and even different books and strings them together as if they were a single passage. Such a cut-and-paste approach could make anyone say anything and Riplinger clearly pays no attention to the context of those whose work she uses.

Even worse, the net effect of her pseudoquotations is to attack the character of other Christians who worked on other Bible translations. It is bad enough to distort someone's words so terribly but to do so in the name of falsely branding them occultists or worse is itself a behavior from which Gail Riplinger needs to repent.

Add to this her mishandling of the Bible itself and you have a mess that confuses the Body of Christ, clouds their judgment, causes unnecessary division among Christians, and leads to an unhealthy view mired in conspiracy theories.

It is astonishing a book so steeped in dishonesty could be accepted so widely by those who claim to follow He who is the Truth. The bizarre claims present in NABV, still with a loyal following among many supporters of KJV Onlyism, is a sickness upon the Church which has been bred from ignorance and has left shattered congregations in its wake. There is no excuse for the followers of Christ to subscribe to the wild

64   Chapter 7 – Conclusion

claims and character assassinations present in *New Age Bible Versions*. The sooner the Church of Christ rids itself of this disorder, the healthier it will be.

Appendix – Book Review

The following is a book review of *New Age Bible Versions* I have written for my website *Christian Book Reviews* (www.christianbookreviews.net):

When reading Gail Riplinger's *New Age Bible Versions*, the question that one must continually ask oneself is this: How did someone read this manuscript and agree to publish it? When originally released, it did create quite the ruckus in Evangelical Protestant circles with many readers becoming convinced that only the King James Version (KJV) of the Bible was the true Word of God. However, once examined by more level heads in the Evangelical community, the controversy generated by the book largely evaporated due to quite straightforward critiques of the quality of Riplinger's research and methodology. Although the book still resonates with some, its appeals is primarily restricted to KJV Only movement whose beliefs seem to reside near the border between fundamentalism and conspiracy theory.

I should point out that as a traditional Anglican I hold the KJV in very high esteem. It is an excellent Bible that has served the Church well for centuries. It stands not only as a reliable text of Holy Scripture but also as one of the greatest literary achievements of the English language. One of the most disturbing aspects of the whole KJV Only movement is its associating the work of those who used their scholarly abilities to advance the Kingdom with the most anti-intellectual elements of the Church.

Riplinger's questionable thesis revolves around the accusation that all available versions of the Bible except the KJV are corrupted and in essence satanic attempts at removing the Christian's main weapon – the Word of God – in the battle against demonic forces. In her attempts to convince the reader, she offers textual comparisons, historic data, biographical information on the translators, voluminous citations and footnotes, and a few techniques unique to her own methods. For those with less than a critical eye and predisposed to see all the problems of the world as arranged by conspirators (as opposed to being a direct result of man's sinful nature), it can be quite convincing.

The problem with Riplinger's analysis is that she – like most conspiracy theorists – simply cannot see outside the box she has created for herself. In her attempts to explain the omissions of certain passages in more recent translations of the Holy Scriptures that appeared in the King James Version, she assumes some nefarious plot behind each variation and never bothers to investigate the reasons for the differences. Much of her argument is predicated upon the alleged superiority of the *Textus Receptus* or received text that was used as the basis for the KJV. However, she has neither the background in Greek or Hebrew nor an understanding of Church history that would allow her to actually contribute anything constructive to the discussion of the manuscript evidence. In place of reason, she simply assumes evil intent on all parties associated with any newer translation and commits wholesale character assassinations against respected Christian scholars. Whatever may be missing from their Bibles, one can only guess that the commandment against bearing false witness must not make an appearance in hers.

Reasons for the differences are quite straightfoward. There are obvious similarities between the texts of the synoptics and with additional information in some variants of the same event. A scribe copying something from Mark (whose descriptions of events were often simpler) may be familiar with the same event in Matthew or Luke and add what he mistakenly thought had been omitted. Many of the so-called "omissions" are of this sort. The text still does appear in a different Gospel but just not in a place where it did not appear originally.

The *Textus Receptus* was based upon the later Byzantine family of texts that is primarily medieval in origin. Other textual families (such as the Alexandrian) are much earlier and their more primitive state is verified by much less polished text. Thus Riplinger's argument that the Byzantine family represented the vast majority of texts is shown to be fallacious. Yes, it is the majority but they are all later texts that do not represent the most primitive form of the texts. The Alexandrian family is earlier and simply a more reliable basis for a translation. The reason for the use of the Byzantine texts was that they were the texts available in the West at the time. The West had until the time of the Reformation had been mainly using the Latin translation by St. Jerome known as the Vulgate. A new translation of the Greek texts into Latin by Erasmus (using a limited number of Byzantine texts) provided the basis for the translation of the KJV. It is ironic that KJV only advocates use arguments against newer translations similar to arguments opposing Erasmus' work because it contradicted parts of the accepted Vulgate translation.

If Riplinger had stuck to arguments on textual families to build a case for the KJV, one could write it off as a well-meaning person in far over her head, but this is simply not the case. She not only questions the use of other texts but also the intentions and even the eternal state of those involved in the newer translations. The most egregious example of this is the treatment of Anglican scholar and bishop B. F. Westcott who with fellow Anglican cleric F. J. A. Hort compiled a standard critical version of the New Testament. The author accuses them of being both deniers of Christ's divinity and closet occultists. The former she asserts by selectively taking quotes from Dr. Westcott and twisting them to mean the exact opposite of their original intent. Her claim of some occultic connection is repeated throughout the book with no supporting evidence. She does mention in a footnote that a Dr. Westcott was associated with Theosophy founder Madame Blavatsky and hypothesizes it was him but that Dr. Westcott was a coroner and known occultist Dr. William Wynn Westcott. Hence, her entire attack is based upon out of context quotes and misidentifications. This is research?

Much of this stuff is common fair on the extreme ends of the fundamentalist landscape but Riplinger does add a few of her own unique contributions. As she explained the "acrostic algebra" that "proves" the

68   Appendix – Book Review

satanic origin of newer translations and her strange fascination with the letter "s", I began to realize that not only is there a fine line between genius and insanity but between stupidity and insanity as well.

I see no problem with someone using the KJV. It is a beautifully written and generally reliable reading of the Bible (as are the other scholarly translations) but has some limitations: archaic words, development in the meaning of words, and the use of later Greek texts. None of these nullify its power as the KJV has been the Bible for millions of Christians through the centuries, but neither does its long history deem it irreplaceable any more than the Vulgate centuries before.

As for New Age Bible Versions, it is not only grossly inaccurate but makes completely unfounded attacks against a number of Christian scholars. Even if one gives Riplinger the benefit of the doubt and assumes both that her misidentification of Dr. Westcott and her misuse of his quotes were appropriated from other secondary sources (this form of unverified "citation borrowing" is rampant among fundamentalist authors), this only indicts her further as one who was willing to use unverified sources to attack a fellow Christian. Even worse, she has made the KJV – once a uniting force among English-speaking Protestants – a source of division. This is a truly onerous book that should have been left unpublished.

Bibliography

Carson, D. A.
The King James Version Debate: A Plea for Realism (Baker Book House, 1978)

Foster, Lewis
Selecting a Translation of the Bible (Standard Publishing, 1983).

Hislop, Alexander
The Two Babylons (Martino Publishing, 2010).

Hort, Arthur Fenton
The Life and Letters of Fenton John Anthony Hort, Volume I (MacMillan and Company, 1896).

Kohlenberger, John R. III
Words About the Word: A Guide to Using and Choosing Your Bible (Regency Reference Library, 1987),

Palmer, Edwin H.
"Isn't the King James Version Good Enough? (The NIV and the KJV Compared)" in ed. Kenneth L. Barker, *The NIV: The Making of a Contemporary Translation* (Academie Books, 1986).

Riplinger, Gail
New Age Bible Versions: An Exhaustive Documentation Exposing the Message, Men, and Manuscripts Moving Mankind to

70 Bibliography

the Antichrist's One World Religion (A.V. Publications, 1999).

Schaff, David Shelby
The Life of Philip Schaff (New York: Charles Scribner's Sons, 1897).

Westcott, Arthur
Life and Letters of Brooke Foss Westcott, Volume I (London, MacMillan and Co., 1903a).
Life and Letters of Brooke Foss Westcott, Volume II (London, MacMillan and Co., 1903b).

Westcott, Brooke Foss
The Christian Life, Manifold and One: Six Sermons Preached in Peterborough Cathedral (MacMillan and Co., 1869).
The Gospel According to St. John: The Authorised Version (John Murray, 1882).
The Historic Faith: Short Lectures on the Apostles' Creed (MacMillan and Co., 1885).
Essays in the History of Religious Thought in the West (MacMillan and Co., 1891a).
Thoughts on Revelation and Life (MacMillan and Co., 1891b).
The Epistles of St. John: The Greek Text with Notes and Essays (MacMillan and Co., 1892).

White, James R.
The King James Only Controversy (Bethany House, 2009).

Woodrow, Ralph
Babylon Mystery Religion (Ralph Woodrow Evangelistic Association, 1979).
The Babylon Connection? (Ralph Woodrow Evangelistic Association, 2004).

Bibliography 71

Printed in Great Britain
by Amazon